INTRODUCTION

Thank you for purchasing Cooking With Gold—your guide to cooking delicious meals with Macadamia nut oil! As a health and fitness professional, my goal was to create a cookbook to help you to improve the quality of your health while eating some great tasting foods!

In the 25-plus years that I have been in the health and fitness industry, I have been astonished that many people think that if a food or meal is healthy, it can't also be delicious. This is possibly a remaining artifact in the collective subconscious of the failed rice-cake diet of 1986. In any event, food should taste good; and food should be enjoyed, while being simultaneously healthy.

Do you like the taste of butter?

For many people the answer is a profound 'yes', 'absolutely' or 'who doesn't?' I agree! However, for many people it's followed by a sense that butter is not healthy. While there have been extensive debates regarding the healthfulness of butter over the years (for the record, I do not believe butter is as bad as many people think). I'm not suggesting it's as healthy as olive oil, but when used occasionally, it could be part of a healthy diet.

Now, wouldn't it be great if there existed something that tasted like butter, but was indeed as healthy as olive oil? Or better yet, even healthier than olive oil (evidence suggests it can be 500% healthier) while retaining a great buttery taste?

Good News.

It does exist. It's called Macadamia Nut Oil. The omega-3 to omega-6 fatty acid ratio is 1:1, which is much better than olive oil, and is good for heart and brain health; but furthermore, the taste is undeniably richer than olive oil.

INTRODUCTION

I began teaching my clients about the benefits of macadamia nut oil initially as a way to improve their diet. It's not uncommon for many individuals to have a diet of highly processed foods, high in bad trans fat while low in good fat. While quality molecularly distilled Fish Oil is indeed the best of these 'good fats', it's not enjoyable nor especially practical for cooking.

So as a way to help my clients achieve results such as lower triglycerides, lower blood pressure, lower blood sugar, lower insulin, greater energy, smoother skin, hair, and nails, and less risk of premature aging, I recommended Macadamia Nut Oil. The positive responses have been incredible!

In addition to the great health benefits, there were some other clear advantages of using macadamia nut oil for cooking. First, is the smoke point. The smoke point of oil is the temperature at which it stops shimmering and starts smoking. The smoke point is also called the burning point of oil and can change the properties of oil from being very healthy and high in omega-3 good fats, to carcinogenic and dangerous.

Fish oil has a low smoke point (90-degrees fahrenheit) which makes it a terrible cooking oil even if you could tolerate the fishy smell and taste. Furthermore, this is the reason that quality fish oil is molecularly distilled at cold temperatures in order to preserve the high omega properties. Olive oil is slightly higher (350-degrees fahrenheit) but still not optimal for high heat cooking.

Macadamia nut oil is very high heat stable. Most indexes list Mac oil at 410-degrees fahrenheit, but I can attest that it can hold up to even higher temperatures. Once my friend and TV chef, Steve Binks, tested mac oil to over 520-degrees without any smoking. This makes it a wonderful cooking, grilling or sauteing oil even at the highest temperatures.

INTRODUCTION

I use mac oil to cook veggies, fish, pork and beef. I even spray it on the grill before I cook chicken to make it non-stick. I also love to use it on the pan when cooking eggs, making it both non-stick and healthy!

Lastly, as I mentioned earlier, it has a rich buttery taste. While olive oil is a great oil, and excellent as a finishing oil on a cold salad, the taste of olive oil is somewhat flat. For many people who remember the low fat/low cholesterol craze between 1980-2000, cooking with olive oil was less than exciting. I can promise you when you use mac oil for most of your cooking you'll deeply enjoy the rich-buttery flavor of many foods.

This might be why Tim Ferriss called Macadamia Nut Oil 'The new olive oil!' in his book, The 4-Hour Body.

Why Australian Macadamia Nut Oil?

Macadamia Nuts are produced primarily in three regions: South Africa, Hawaii, and Australia. South Africa is home to the largest acreage of macadamia nuts and the refineries produce the largest yield of oil. Hawaii also has significant acreage, however the macadamia nut is not indigenous to Hawaii. rather it was brought over from Australia and planted in the 1890s. Macadamia nuts are indigenous to Australia. Because of this, some believe that because of the perfect soil conditions the nut has the best tasting buttery flavor and aroma. Honestly, my experience has always supported that Australia produces the best tasting of all macadamia nut oils. South African oil tastes burnt and Hawaiian oil tastes thin and watery.

In addition, the refinery processes of Australia are one of the toughest and heavily regulated for cold-pressing quality standards.

The cold-press process means the oil obtained needs to be from grinding the nut with a heavy granite millstone or stainless steel press.

This process produces heat through friction which ruins the beneficial omega 3 properties of the nut. Unfortunately, many refineries practice this process due to economic reasons. Luckily, the Australian Government demands the temperature not exceed 49 degrees Celsius in the cold-pressing process. This helps ensure the best possible health properties for the consumer. That is the reason why many research scientists and nutritionists believe Australia cold pressed macadamia nut oil is the best and healthiest in the world

I strongly suggest you try the recipes I have included on the following pages. They are designed with a healthy, lower carb, low glycemic index, even Keto-friendly approach. They are great for anyone looking to improve their health and fitness. If you do not currently have low carb or healthier goals, you can still use this oil with your favorite dishes to enjoy the versatility and taste of the oil.

You might think that you're cooking with butter - but this is healthier for sure!

Enjoy,

Dr. Derek Alessi
Ph.D.

TABLE OF CONTENTS

BREAKFAST

BACON & AVOCADO OMELET

INGREDIENTS:

- 3 eggs

- 3 tablespoons bell pepper, chopped

- 3 tablespoons red onion, chopped

- 3 tablespoons cheddar cheese, shredded

- 3 tablespoons asiago cheese, shredded

- 3 pieces cooked bacon

- 5 mushrooms, sliced

- 8-10 slices of avocado

- Chopped parsley, to taste

- Salt & pepper, to taste

- 2 tablespoons Strength Genesis Mac Oil

- 2 tablespoons of water or heavy cream

BACON & AVOCADO OMELET

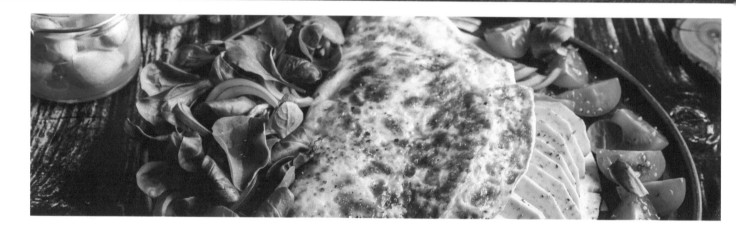

DIRECTIONS:

- In a large skillet, heat the Mac oil over medium heat. Saute the pepper and onion for 3-5 minutes.

- Add mushrooms and saute for another 3-5 minutes. Remove vegetables from the pan and set aside.

- Whisk together eggs, salt, pepper, and water or cream.

- Heat more Mac oil in the skillet, and slowly pour the egg mixture into the pan. Turn the heat to medium-low.

- As eggs set, lift edges and allow uncooked egg to flow into the open spaces.

- Once egg is almost fully cooked, sprinkle the surface with asiago cheese and parsley.

- Place sauteed vegetables onto one side of the eggs, top with cheddar cheese, cooked bacon and avocado slices.

- Fold the eggs over the top of the toppings and serve immediately.

TURKEY & VEGGIE OMELET

INGREDIENTS:

- 3 eggs
- 1 tablespoon water
- 1 teaspoon Strength Genesis Mac Oil
- ¼ cup turkey sausage
- ¼ cup bell pepper, chopped
- 2 tablespoons onion, chopped
- ¼ cup spinach, chopped
- 2 tablespoons cheddar cheese, shredded
- Salt & pepper, to taste

TURKEY & VEGGIE OMELET

DIRECTIONS:

- Whisk together eggs, water, salt and pepper, set aside.

- In an 8-inch pan, over medium heat, cook sausage, pepper and onion until sausage is cooked through and onion is translucent. Add spinach and heat until wilted. Empty contents of pan onto a plate and set aside.

- Add Mac oil to the pan, once oil is hot, slowly add egg mixture to the pan. Allow eggs to cook for about 30 seconds, then begin lifting the edges and allow the runny eggs to fill in the gaps. Cook for another 30 seconds, or until the eggs are cooked enough to be flipped.

- Turn off the heat, flip the eggs carefully. Place half of the cheese on one side of the eggs, add the vegetables, and top with the second half of the cheese.

- Fold the egg over onto the side with the toppings, allow to sit for one minute and serve.

STEAK OMELET

INGREDIENTS:

- 3 large eggs

- Salt & pepper, to taste

- 1 grilled steak, diced

- 2 baby bella mushrooms, sliced

- 1 roma tomato, diced

- Pepper jack cheese, to taste

- Hot sauce, to taste

- Green onions for garnish

- Strength Genesis Mac Oil

DIRECTIONS:

- Whisk together eggs, water, salt and pepper, set aside.

- In an 8-inch pan, heat Mac oil over medium-high heat.

- Once oil is hot, reduce the heat to medium and slowly add egg mixture to the pan. Allow eggs to cook for about 30 seconds, then begin lifting the edges and allowing the runny eggs to fill in the gaps. Cook for another 30 seconds, or until the eggs are cooked enough to be flipped.

- Turn off the heat, flip the eggs carefully. Place half of the cheese on one side of the eggs, add the vegetables and steak, and top with the second half of the cheese.

- Fold the egg over onto the side with the toppings, allow to sit for one minute and serve topped with hot sauce and green onions.

CRUSTLESS HAM QUICHE

INGREDIENTS:

- 1 cup cooked ham, diced
- 1 cup zucchini, shredded
- 1 cup cheddar cheese, shredded
- 8 large eggs
- ½ cup heavy cream
- ½ teaspoon dry mustard
- Salt & pepper, to taste

CRUSTLESS HAM QUICHE

DIRECTIONS:

- Preheat the oven to 375 degrees.

- Prepare a 9" pie plate by brushing or spraying it with Strength Genesis Mac Oil.

- Place zucchini onto paper towel and squeeze to remove moisture.

- Combine ham, zucchini and cheese in the pie plate.

- Whisk eggs, cream and seasoning together and pour over the other ingredients.

- Bake uncovered for 40 minutes, until a fork can be inserted and come out clean.

GREEK BREAKFAST SCRAMBLE

INGREDIENTS:

- 10 large eggs

- ⅔ cup feta cheese, crumbled

- ¼ cup heavy cream

- Salt & pepper, to taste

- 1 tablespoon Strength Genesis Mac Oil

- ½ medium yellow onion, diced

- 5-6 oz. baby spinach

- 1 cup cherry tomatoes, quartered

GREEK BREAKFAST SCRAMBLE

DIRECTIONS:

- Whisk together egg, cream, feta, salt and pepper, and set aside.

- Heat Mac oil in a large skillet or seasoned cast iron skillet over medium heat. Once oil is hot, add onions and salt and cook until soft. Add spinach and cook until wilted and liquid is evaporated.

- Reduce heat to medium-low and pour egg mixture into the skillet. Allow eggs to sit on the heat for about 30 seconds, or until the edges of the eggs begin to set. Begin pushing the cooked eggs inwards and allowing the uncooked egg to run towards the edges.

- Continue this process about every 30 seconds until the eggs are cooked, but still slightly wet.

- Remove the eggs from the heat, fold in the tomatoes, and serve immediately.

SAUSAGE FRITTATA

INGREDIENTS:

- 1 lb ground sausage

- 8 eggs, beaten

- ½ cup bell pepper, diced

- ½ cup white onion, diced

- ½ cup Parmesan shredded

- 2 tablespoons fresh parsley, chopped

- ½ cup heavy cream

- 2 tablespoons Strength Genesis Mac Oil

SAUSAGE FRITTATA

DIRECTIONS:

- Preheat oven to 425 degrees.

- Heat Mac oil in a large, oven safe skillet over medium heat.

- Add pepper, onion and sausage to the pan and cook and crumple the sausage for 5-8 minutes, until the sausage is cooked through.

- Whisk together eggs, cream, parsley and cheese. Pour the mixture over the other ingredients in the skillet. Cook for 2-3 minutes.

- Remove the skillet from the stove and place it in the preheated oven. Bake for 20-30 minutes, until the eggs are set in the center.

- Cut into pieces and serve

ENTREES

THAI GRILLED CHICKEN

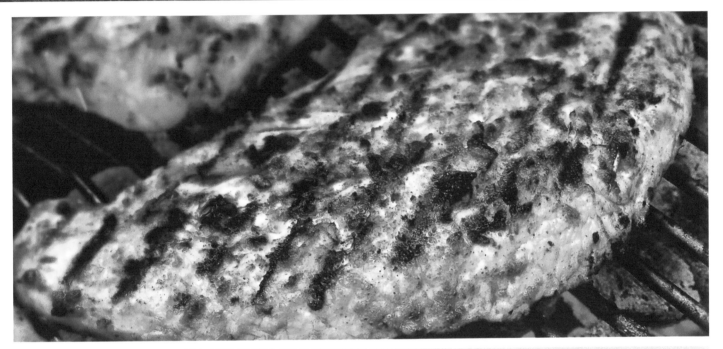

INGREDIENTS:

- 2 lbs. boneless, skinless chicken thighs
- Thai Marinade
- Salt and freshly ground black pepper
- Garnish optional:
- Lettuce
- Cucumber cut into strips
- Green onions
- Limes, quartered
- 1 tsp. ground pepper

THAI MARINADE:

- 1 tsp. ground cumin
- 2 Tbsp. sugar or equivalent substitute
- 1 Tbsp. paprika
- ½ inch piece ginger root, chopped
- 4 cloves garlic, minced
- ½ oz. cilantro, finely chopped
- 3 Tbsp. garlic infused* Strength Genesis Mac Oil

THAI GRILLED CHICKEN

DIRECTIONS:

- Score chicken pieces lightly on each side to allow the marinade to penetrate.

- Combine the ingredients for the marinade.

- Spread the marinade over the chicken and refrigerate for 6 hours or overnight.

- Cook the chicken on a medium heat for 15 to 20 minutes, basting with the marinade and turning once. Arrange on a bed of lettuce and garnish with cucumber, green onions and limes, if desired. Makes 6 servings.

- *for instructions on how to infuse mac oil see page 62

KOREAN TERI CHICKEN

INGREDIENTS:

- 2 cups soy sauce
- 1 cup sugar
- 1 large thumb ginger
- 3 1/2 Tbsp. garlic infused* Strength Genesis Mac Oil
- 1/2 Tbsp. sesame oil
- 1 tsp. red chili pepper
- 1 Tbsp. toasted sesame seeds
- 8 chicken thighs
- Green onions thinly sliced for garnish

DIRECTIONS

- Combine all ingredients, except chicken and green onions; blend well.
- Add chicken and marinate for 1 to 2 hours.
- Grill on medium heat until cooked through, flipping for even cooking. Garnish with green onions. Makes 4 servings.
- *for instructions on how to infuse mac oil see page 62

TUSCAN GRILLED STEAK

INGREDIENTS:

- 2 16 oz. steaks
- 4 tablespoons Strength Genesis Mac Oil
- Zest of 1 lemon
- 2 cloves of garlic, minced
- 1 teaspoon fresh rosemary
- ¼ teaspoon dried thyme
- ½ teaspoon red pepper flake
- Ground black pepper to taste

DIRECTIONS

- In a large Ziploc bag, combine all ingredients and massage to ensure the steaks are covered in marinade.
- Marinade for 12 hours.
- Preheat grill to 450 degrees.
- Grill steaks for 2-3 minutes per side for medium-rare steak, or cook to your desired temperature.

GRILLED GREEK CHICKEN SKEWERS

INGREDIENTS:

- ½ cup full fat, plain greek yogurt
- ¼ cup Strength Genesis Mac Oil
- ¼ cup fresh lemon juice
- Zest of 1 lemon
- 1 tablespoon white balsamic vinegar
- 2 tablespoons fresh oregano, chopped
- 1 tablespoon fresh thyme
- 6 medium garlic cloves, minced
- 1 teaspoon salt
- 1 teaspoon pepper
- ¼ teaspoon red pepper flakes
- 3-4 boneless, skinless chicken breasts, cut into 2-inch pieces
- 1 red bell pepper, seeded and cubed
- 1 medium red onion, cubed
- 6-8 skewers

GRILLED GREEK CHICKEN SKEWERS

DIRECTIONS:

- In a large Ziploc bag, combine all ingredients except for the chicken and vegetables. Seal the bag and massage it to ensure the ingredients are mixed well.

- Add chicken to the bag, seal, and turn to coat. Marinate for 4-24 hours, turning the bag occasionally while marinating.

- Preheat grill to 400 degrees.

- Pour the marinated chicken into a strainer to remove excess marinade. Thread chicken, peppers and onion on skewers. Grill 4 minutes on each side until chicken is cooked and juices run clear.

JUICY STOVETOP CHICKEN

INGREDIENTS:

- 5 tablespoons Strength Genesis Mac Oil

- 4 boneless, skinless chicken breasts (1 inch thick)

- Salt and pepper to taste

- ½ teaspoon garlic powder

- ½ teaspoon onion powder

- ½ teaspoon dried basil

- ½ teaspoon smoked or sweet paprika

JUICY STOVETOP CHICKEN

DIRECTIONS:

- In a large skillet (10-12 inch), heat 1 ½ tablespoons of Mac oil over medium high heat.

- Pat chicken breasts dry with paper towel and drizzle with Mac oil to lightly coat them.

- In a small bowl, mix salt, pepper, garlic powder, onion powder, basil and paprika.

- Rub the spice mix evenly onto all sides of each chicken breast.

- Add 2 chicken breasts to to the skillet and cook for 5-7 minutes. Flip the chicken and add about 1 tablespoon of oil. Continue cooking for 5-7 minutes or until the chicken is cooking through.

- Remove the chicken from the skillet to rest and repeat the process with the other two chicken breasts.

- Serve immediately.

SEABASS WITH AVOCADO SALSA

INGREDIENTS:

- 4 portions sea bass

- 3 tablespoons Strength Genesis Mac Oil

- 2 teaspoons soy sauce

- ½ teaspoon ground ginger

- 2 large avocados, diced

- 1 teaspoon jalapeno, minced

- 2 tablespoons fresh cilantro, chopped

- Juice of 1 lime

- Salt to taste

- Red pepper flakes to taste (optional)

SEABASS WITH AVOCADO SALSA

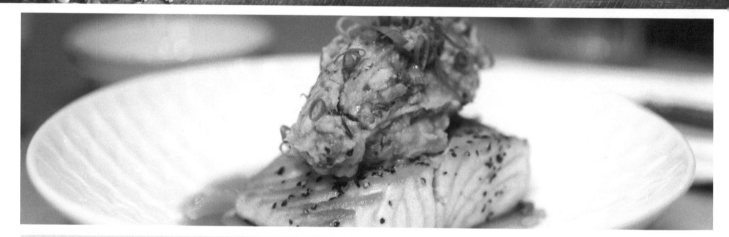

DIRECTIONS:

- In a small bowl, combine avocado, jalapeno, cilantro and 2 tablespoons of lime juice. Mix together and put aside.

- In a small bowl, whisk together 2 tablespoons of Mac oil, soy sauce, ginger and remaining lime juice.

- Place the sea bass into a shallow dish and pour the marinade over it, flipping the fish to coat it completely. Refrigerate until ready to cook, no more than 15-20 minutes.

- Spray or brush a large skillet with Mac oil and heat the skillet over medium-high heat.

- Add the fish to the skillet and cook for about 4 minutes per side, until the fish is fully cooked and flaky.

- Remove the fish from the skillet and serve immediately topped with avocado salsa.

LEMON GARLIC SWORDFISH

INGREDIENTS:

- 4 tablespoons Strength Genesis Mac Oil
- 1 tablespoon fresh chives, chopped
- 2 tablespoon, garlic, minced
- ⅛ teaspoon salt
- ¼ teaspoon ground black pepper
- 1 tablespoon lemon juice
- 1 tablespoon lemon zest
- 2 swordfish fillets

LEMON GARLIC SWORDFISH

DIRECTIONS:

- In a small pot, combine 2 tablespoons of Mac oil, chives, garlic, salt, pepper, lemon juice and lemon zest. Set aside.

- Preheat oven to 400 degrees.

- Pat the swordfish dry using a paper towel, and sprinkle salt and pepper evenly onto both sides of the fillets.

- Heat the remaining Mac oil in an oven-safe skillet over medium heat. Once hot, add the fillets to the skillet and cook for 3 minutes, or until one side is brown.

- Flip the fish and immediately transfer the skillet into the oven. Roast the fish for 5-6 minutes, or until the fish is cooked through.

- While the fish is roasting, heat the already mixed sauce until it is warm and slightly bubbling.

- Remove the fish from the oven and serve immediately topped with the lemon garlic sauce.

SPICY SHRIMP

INGREDIENTS:

- 1 pound large shrimp (16-20 count)

- 1/2 cup Strength Genesis Mac Oil

- 2 Tbsp. Cajun or Creole seasoning

- 2 Tbsp. fresh lemon juice

- 1 Tbsp. soy sauce

- 1/2 Tbsp. honey

- 2 cloves garlic, minced

- 2 Tbsp. chopped cilantro

- Lemon wedges for garnish

- French bread, thinly slice

SPICY SHRIMP

DIRECTIONS:

- Peel shells from shrimp, leaving tails attached, and remove the veins.

- Combine macadamia oil, Cajun seasoning, lemon juice, soy sauce, honey, garlic and cilantro; pour over shrimp.

- Refrigerate at least 1 hour.

- Preheat oven to 450°F. Bake until shrimp are cooked through, about 8 to 10 minutes.

- Garnish with lemon wedges.

- Makes 4 servings.

LEMON CHICKEN WITH BROCCOLI

INGREDIENTS:

- 3-4 boneless, skinless chicken breast

- 3 cups broccoli florets

- 1 cup chicken broth

- ¼ cup lemon juice (about ½ lemon, juiced)

- 1 tablespoon Strength Genesis Mac Oil

- ½ tablespoon garlic, minced

- ½ teaspoon onion powder

- ½ teaspoon chili powder

- Salt and pepper to taste

LEMON CHICKEN WITH BROCCOLI

DIRECTIONS:

- Heat Mac oil in a large skillet.

- Season both sides of chicken breast with onion powder, chili powder, salt and pepper and add to the skillet.

- Pour or squeeze lemon juice onto chicken. Cook chicken 5 minutes on each side.

- Add broccoli, garlic, and chicken broth to skillet. Cook for 10 more minutes, stirring broccoli occasionally and flipping chicken at least once, until it is cooked through.

- Top with parsley and lemon juice before serving if desired.

LEMON GARLIC 'BUTTER" CHICKEN & GREEN BEAN SKILLET

INGREDIENTS:

- 3-6 boneless, skinless chicken thighs (or chicken breast)
- 1 lb green beans, trimmed
- 3 tablespoons Strength Genesis Mac Oil
- 4 cloves garlic, minced
- 1 tablespoon hot sauce
- 1 teaspoon paprika
- 1 teaspoon onion powder
- Salt and pepper to taste
- Juice of ½ a lemon
- ½ cup chicken broth
- ½ cup fresh chopped parsley
- Red pepper flakes, to taste (optional)

LEMON GARLIC 'BUTTER' CHICKEN & GREEN BEAN SKILLET

DIRECTIONS:

- In a small bowl, combine spices. Season the chicken evenly on both sides and set aside.

- In a microwave safe bowl, combine green beans and ½ cup of water and cook in the microwave for 8-10 minutes. The green beans should be almost cooked but still crisp.

- Heat 2 tablespoons of Mac oil in a large skillet on medium-low heat. Add chicken to skillet in a single layer. Allow the chicken to cook for 5-6 minutes per side and continue flipping it until it is cooked through. Once cooked through, remove chicken from skillet and set aside.

- Lower the cooking heat and add the remaining Mac oil to the same skillet. Add parsley, hot sauce, garlic and green beans to the skillet and cook for 5-6 minutes, stirring occasionally. Add lemon juice and chicken broth and reduce for a few minutes, allowing the liquid to thicken.

- Add the chicken back to the pan to reheat and serve immediately.

BLACKENED
SALMON

INGREDIENTS:

- 4 4 oz. salmon fillets (skin on)

- 4 tablespoons Strength Genesis Mac Oil

- 2 teaspoons smoked paprika

- 1 teaspoon chili powder

- 1 teaspoon salt

- 1 teaspoon dried oregano

- 1 teaspoon dried thyme

- ½ teaspoon onion powder

- ½ teaspoon black pepper

- Cayenne pepper to taste

BLACKENED SALMON

DIRECTIONS:

- In a small bowl, mix together spices and set aside.

- Pat salmon dry with a paper towel.

- Coat the fleshy side of the salmon with Mac oil and sprinkle with spice mixture, using your fingers to ensure the spices adhere to the fish.

- Heat a cast iron skillet over medium heat and add Mac oil to the pan. Add the salmon fillets to the skillet, flesh side down, and allow to cook for 2-3 minutes, until the spices are toasted and dark.

- Flip the salmon, skin side down, and cook for 5-6 minutes, adding a bit more Mac oil to help the skin become crisp. The salmon should be opaque and flaky when done. Serve immediately.

GRILLED CHICKEN & AVOCADO SALSA

INGREDIENTS:

- 1 ½ lb boneless, skinless chicken breast (about 4 chicken breasts)
- 2 cloves of garlic, minced
- 3 tablespoons of Strength Genesis Mac Oil
- 2 avocados
- 2 small (or 1 large) tomatoes, diced
- ¼ cup red onion, chopped
- 1 jalapeno, seeded and chopped (optional)
- ½ cup cilantro, finely chopped
- Juice of 2 limes
- ½ teaspoon of cumin
- ½ teaspoon of paprika
- Salt & pepper to taste

GRILLED CHICKEN & AVOCADO SALSA

DIRECTIONS:

- In a bowl, whisk together Mac oil, garlic, ¼ cup cilantro, cumin, paprika, salt, pepper and the juice of 1 lime, set aside.

- Pound chicken breasts to an even thickness and cut in horizontally in half if necessary. Add chicken to marinade and mix until all chicken is coated. Marinate for 30 minutes to 12 hours.

- Grill chicken on medium-high heat for 5-6 minutes per side or until cooked through and there is slight charring on the outside. Remove from heat and top with avocado salsa, serve immediately.

- To make the salsa: in a separate bowl, combine avocado, tomato, onion, jalapeno, ¼ cup cilantro, salt, pepper, and the juice of one lime. Refrigerate until ready to serve.

Sheet Pan Chicken Fajitas

INGREDIENTS:

- 1 ½ lbs boneless, skinless, chicken breast tenders
- 1 yellow bell pepper, sliced
- 1 orange bell pepper, sliced
- 1 small red onion, sliced
- 1 ½ tablespoons of Strength Genesis Mac Oil
- 1 teaspoon sea salt
- Freshly ground pepper, to taste
- 2 teaspoons chili powder

- ½ teaspoon garlic powder
- ½ teaspoon onion powder
- ½ teaspoon ground cumin
- ½ teaspoon smoked paprika

Sheet Pan Chicken Fajitas

DIRECTIONS:

- Preheat oven to 425 degrees.

- In a large bowl, combine onion, pepper, chicken, Mac oil and spices. Toss to combine.

- Brush or spray baking sheet with a thin layer of Mac oil. Spread the chicken, onion and peppers in a single layer on the baking sheet.

- Bake for 20 minutes or until the chicken is cooked through. Broil for the last 1-2 minutes, using care not to burn the vegetables.

- If desired, sprinkle with lime juice and cilantro and serve immediately.

ENTREES

CAESAR SALAD

INGREDIENTS

- 1 head Romaine lettuce

- 1/2 cup Mac Oil Caesar Dressing (see recipe below)

- Croutons, optional

- Grated Parmesan cheese to sprinkle

MAC OIL CAESAR DRESSING

- 1/4 cup Strength Genesis Mac Oil

- 1 can (2 oz.) anchovies, drained

- 2 Tbsp. lemon juice or white wine vinegar

- 1 tsp. sugar or equivalent sugar substitute

- 1/2 cup mayonnaise

- 1/4 cup grated Parmesan cheese

- 2 cloves garlic, minced

- 1/4 tsp. Dijon mustard

- In a food processor combine macadamia oil and anchovies; pulse several times to mash. Add lemon juice and sugar and pulse a few more times. Add all the remaining ingredients and blend well. Chill. Makes about 3/4 cup.

DIRECTIONS:

- Preheat oven to 425 degrees.

- In a large bowl, combine onion, pepper, chicken, Mac oil and spices. Toss to combine.

- Brush or spray baking sheet with a thin layer of Mac Oil. Spread the chicken, onion and peppers in a single layer on the baking sheet.

- Bake for 20 minutes or until the chicken is cooked through. Broil for the last 1-2 minutes, using care not to burn the vegetables.

- If desired, sprinkle with lime juice and cilantro and serve immediately.

MACADAMIA HUMMUS

INGREDIENTS:

- 1 can (15 1/2 oz.) garbanzo beans, drain and reserve liquid
- 1/3 cup tahini
- 1/4 cup garlic infused* Strength Genesis Mac Oil
- 1/4 cup fresh lemon juice
- 1 1/2 tsp. ground cumin

DIRECTIONS

- In a food processor combine garbanzo beans, tahini, Mac oil, lemon juice and cumin. Purée the ingredients, slowly adding the reserved liquid from the garbanzo beans, until mixture is a smooth paste. Chill and serve as a dip for vegetables. Makes 2 cups.
- *for instructions on how to infuse mac oil see page 62

GRILLED ZUCCHINI

INGREDIENTS:

- 2 medium zucchinis
- 1 lemon, zested and juiced
- 2 tablespoons Strength Genesis Mac Oil
- Salt & pepper, to taste

DIRECTIONS

- Preheat your oven to high heat.
- Slice zucchini ¼ inch thick ovals and toss with the rest of the ingredients.
- Place the zucchini slices in a single layer directly onto the grill surface and cook for approx. 3 minutes, until grill marks appear on the zucchini. Reserve the oil and lemon juice mixture.
- Carefully flip the zucchini slices and repeat the process.
- Once cooked through, remove the zucchini from the grill and drizzle with the reserved oil and lemon juice. Serve immediately.

GRILLED BRUSSEL SPROUTS

INGREDIENTS:

- 1 lb brussel sprouts, halved
- 2-3 tablespoons Strength Genesis Mac Oil
- Salt and pepper to taste
- ¼ cup fresh parmesan
- Wooden skewers

DIRECTIONS

- Soak wooden skewers in water for at least 30 minutes
- Preheat grill to medium heat.
- Bring a large pot of water to a boil, add brussel sprouts and cook for 3 minutes. Drain and rinse with cold water.
- Thread the brussel sprouts onto the wooden skewers. Brush the sprouts with Mac oil, and sprinkle with salt and pepper.
- Place the skewers on the grill and cook for 5-7 minutes per side, until cooked to preference.

GRILLED PEPPERS

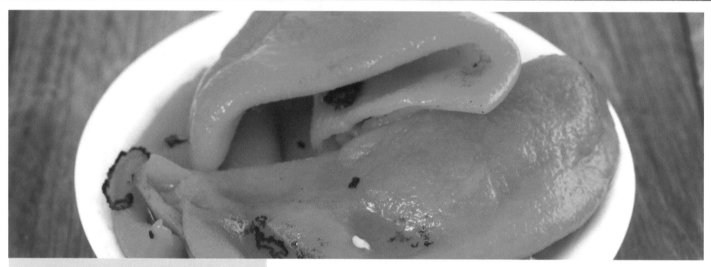

INGREDIENTS:

- 3 medium bell peppers
- 2-3 cloves of garlic, minced
- ½ cup parsley, chopped
- ¼ cup Strength Genesis Mac Oil
- ½ teaspoon salt

DIRECTIONS

- Preheat grill to high heat.
- Place the peppers on the grill top and allow to blister, continuously turn the peppers for even cooking.
- Once each pepper is a bit 'burnt' all over, remove them from the heat and place into a brown paper bag or glass bowl covered in plastic and let them sit for 15-20 minutes.
- Remove seeds from the peppers and cut them into strips, and add the strips into a bowl. Add the rest of the ingredients and mix well. Allow the mix to sit for 30-60 minutes and serve.

ROASTED VEGETABLE MEDLEY

INGREDIENTS:

- 3 zucchini squash, chopped
- 3 yellow squash, chopped
- 1 red bell pepper, chopped
- 1 red onion, cut into wedges
- 1 package whole mushrooms
- 1 clove garlic, minced
- 1 tablespoon balsamic vinegar
- 1 tablespoon Strength Genesis Mac Oil
- 1 tablespoon rosemary leaves
- 1 tablespoon salt

DIRECTIONS

- Preheat oven to 450 degrees.
- In a large bowl, mix together all cut vegetables and garlic. Add vinegar and Mac oil and toss until all vegetables are coated.
- Add rosemary and salt and toss again.
- Transfer the vegetables to a baking sheet greased with Mac oil and roast for 30-40 minutes, stirring once.
- Cook until vegetables are slightly browned and tender.

GARLIC PARMESEAN BROCCOLI

INGREDIENTS:

- 24 oz. broccoli florets, fresh or thawed
- 3 tablespoons Strength Genesis Mac Oil
- 3 teaspoons garlic, minced
- Salt, to taste
- ¼ cup parmesan cheese, shredded

DIRECTIONS

- Preheat the oven to 425 degrees.
- Spray or brush a baking sheet with Mac oil.
- In a large bowl, combine broccoli, garlic, Mac oil and salt. Toss until broccoli is completely coated.
- Spread the broccoli in a single layer on the baking sheet. Drizzle excess oil and garlic in the bowl on top.
- Back for 10-12 minutes, or until broccoli is cooking through.
- Sprinkle cooked broccoli with parmesan before serving.

ROASTED GARLIC MAC ASPARAGUS

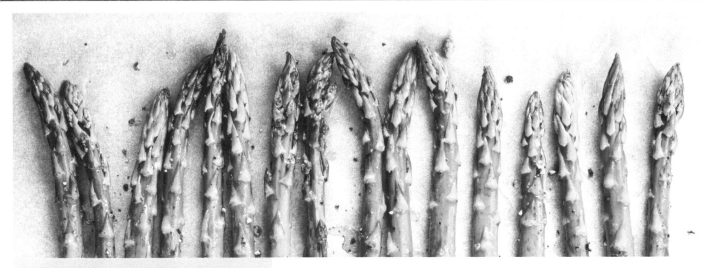

INGREDIENTS:

- 1 lb. asparagus
- 2 Tbsp. garlic infused* Strength Genesis Mac Oil
- 1/2 tsp. coarse sea salt

DIRECTIONS

- Preheat oven to 375°F. Rinse asparagus and snap off the bottoms of the stalks.
- Place asparagus in a foil lined roasting pan. Drizzle with Mac oil and sprinkle with salt. Roast for 8 to 10 minutes or until spears are tender when pierced with a fork. Makes 6 servings.
- *for instructions on how to infuse mac oil see page 62

ROASTED GARLIC

INGREDIENTS:

- 8 whole garlic bulbs
- 2/3 cup Strength Genesis Mac Oil
- 2 Tbsp. chopped fresh thyme or 2 teaspoons dried thyme
- 1 tsp. coarsely cracked black pepper
- 1/2 tsp. coarse sea salt
- 3/4 cup beef or chicken stock

DIRECTIONS

- Preheat oven to 350°F. Remove outer papery skin from garlic bulbs, but do not separate or peel the individual cloves.
- Cut a thin slice off the top of each bulb. Place garlic in a small baking dish. Drizzle with Mac oil. Top with thyme, black pepper and sea salt. Add stock.
- Cover and bake, basting occasionally with stock, for 1 hour. Uncover and bake until garlic is very tender, about 15 minutes more.
- Serve the garlic in the baking dish and press the roasted garlic cloves from their skins and spread like butter. Use cooking liquid as dip, if desired. Makes 12 servings.

MUFFELETTA SPREAD

INGREDIENTS:

- 2/3 cup pitted green olives
- 2/3 cup pitted black olives
- Zest of 1 small orange
- Zest of 1 small lemon
- 2 anchovy filets, mashed
- 1/4 cup pimentos, chopped
- 6 sprigs Italian parsley, chopped
- 1 tsp. oregano
- 1/4 tsp. ground black pepper
- 1/2 cup garlic infused* Strength Genesis Mac Oil

DIRECTIONS

- Coarsely chop the olives and place in a bowl.
- Chop the zest and add to the olives. Stir in all of the remaining ingredients; blend well. Cover and chill for at least 12 hours. Serve with your favorite raw veggies for dipping.
- Makes about 2 cups.
- *for instructions on how to infuse mac oil see page 62

EXTRAS

MAC OIL PESTO

BASIL PESTO INGREDIENTS:

- 1 cup basil leaves
- ¼ cup Strength Genesis Mac Oil
- ¼ cup pine nuts*
- 1 oz. parmesan

ARUGULA-THYME PESTO INGREDIENTS:

- 1 cup baby arugula
- ¼ cup thyme leaves
- ¼ cup Strength Genesis Mac Oil
- ¼ cup pistachios*
- 1 clove garlic

CILANTRO-PARSLEY PESTO INGREDIENTS:

- 1 cup cilantro
- 1 cup parsley
- 2 tablespoons almonds, blanched & sliced*
- Juice of ½ a lemon
- ¼ cup Strength Genesis Mac Oil
- ½ teaspoon salt

MAC OIL PESTO

SAGE PESTO INGREDIENTS:

- 1 cup sage
- ¼ cup Strength Genesis Mac Oil
- ¼ cup pine nuts*
- ½ teaspoon salt
- 1 clove garlic

INGREDIENTS:

- Combine all ingredients in a food processor, blend until desired consistency, and serve on your favorite dish of any kind.
- *Since Mac oil has a nutty taste, the nuts may not be needed in your pesto! Keep them in the recipe for texture or go without and still enjoy incredible flavor.

GARLIC INFUSED MAC OIL

Infuse 1 whole clove of garlic, peeled, per 1 cup of Strength Genesis Mac Oil. Leave to marinate for at least 2 hours. Refrigerate infused oil for up to 2 days.

You may also enjoy some of our other incredible products!

Origin Salad Dressing and Marinade

Pur-Zealand Grass Fed Whey Powder

Omega 3 Molecularly Distilled, Cold Pressed Fish Oil